DO IT, DON'T DELAY

DILEEP KUMAR DAS

To all those who are committed to personal growth and transformation, who have the courage to face their fears, the resilience to overcome their challenges, and the wisdom to embrace their full potential.

To all those who seek to live a life of purpose and meaning, to cultivate their strengths, to connect with others, and to create a positive impact in the world.

To all those who inspire us with their stories, their insights, and their example, who remind us that we are all capable of greatness, and who challenge us to be our best selves.

To my family, my friends, my mentors, and my readers, who have supported and encouraged me on my own journey of self-discovery, and who have taught me the power of love, compassion, and community.

This book is dedicated to you. May it inspire, guide, and support you on your path to self-mastery, and may you continue to grow and thrive in all areas of your life.

Contents

Foreword

As human beings, we all have an innate desire to grow, improve, and become the best version of ourselves. Yet, many of us struggle to find the resources, guidance, and support we need to make that journey of self-discovery.

That's why I'm thrilled to introduce this book on self-development, a comprehensive guide to help you navigate the path of personal growth and transformation. Written with clarity, insight, and compassion, this book offers a wealth of practical tools, strategies, and exercises to help you cultivate the skills and mindset you need to achieve your goals, overcome your fears, and live a life of purpose and meaning.

Whether you are a student, a professional, an entrepreneur, or simply someone who wants to live a more fulfilling life, this book will provide you with the guidance, inspiration, and support you need to succeed. From developing a growth mindset to building healthy habits, from cultivating self-compassion to improving your communication skills, from setting and achieving meaningful goals to creating a positive and supportive environment, this book offers a holistic approach to self-development that can help you thrive in all areas of your life.

As a reader of this book, you will not only gain valuable insights and strategies, but you will also join a community of like-minded individuals who share your commitment to personal growth and transformation. Whether you are reading this book on your own or as part of a study group, you will find a wealth of resources and support to help you on your journey.

So, I invite you to embark on this journey of self-discovery with an open mind and an open heart. May this book serve as a source of inspiration, guidance, and support on your path to self-mastery.

Preface

<u>introduction of the book</u>

Dear Reader,

I wrote this book because I believe that each and every one of us has the potential to live a fulfilling, joyful, and meaningful life. But all too often, we get stuck in patterns of thinking, feeling, and behaving that hold us back from realizing our full potential.

This book is my attempt to share what I've learned about how to overcome these obstacles and create a life that feels authentic, purposeful, and joyful. Whether you're struggling with anxiety, self-doubt, relationship issues, or simply a sense of feeling stuck, my hope is that the insights and strategies contained in this book will help you to break free from old patterns and create a new, more empowered way of being.

Of course, I'm not suggesting that this book contains all the answers. Each of us is unique, and what works for one person may not work for another. But my hope is that the ideas and practices I've shared here will serve as a starting point for your own journey of self-discovery and personal growth.

Thank you for choosing to read this book. I hope that it will be a valuable resource for you as you move forward on your path.

With warmest regards, DILEEP KUMAR DAS.

Acknowledgements

Writing a book is a journey, and I am grateful for the many people who have supported and inspired me along the way.

To my family, thank you for your unwavering love and support, for believing in me, and for encouraging me to follow my dreams.

To my friends, thank you for your encouragement, your feedback, and your enthusiasm for this project. Your support has been invaluable.

To my mentors and teachers, thank you for your guidance, your wisdom, and your inspiration. You have challenged me to grow and learn, and I am grateful for the lessons you have taught me.

To my readers, thank you for your interest in this book, and for allowing me to be a part of your journey of self-discovery. It is my hope that this book will inspire and guide you in your pursuit of personal growth and transformation.

To the team at the publisher, thank you for your hard work, your dedication, and your passion for this project. Your expertise and support have made this book possible.

Finally, I want to acknowledge all those who have come before me, who have shared their wisdom, their insights, and their experience on the path of self-discovery. This book stands on the shoulders of giants, and I am grateful for the opportunity to contribute to this rich tradition of personal growth and transformation.

Thank you all.

Prologue

We all want to be the best versions of ourselves, to live a life that is fulfilling, purposeful, and meaningful. Yet, the journey of personal growth can be both challenging and rewarding. It requires us to confront our fears, to break through limiting beliefs, and to step outside our comfort zones.

This book is a guide to help you on that journey. It is a collection of insights, tools, and practices that can help you develop the skills and mindset you need to achieve your goals, improve your relationships, and live a more satisfying life.

Through the pages of this book, you will discover the power of self-awareness, learn how to set and achieve meaningful goals, and develop the resilience and resourcefulness needed to overcome obstacles and challenges. You will also find practical strategies to improve your communication skills, deepen your connections with others, and create a more positive and supportive environment for yourself and those around you.

This book is not a quick fix or a magic bullet. It is a journey, and the path is different for each of us. But if you are willing to take that journey, if you are committed to your growth and development, this book can be your guide and companion on the path to self-mastery.

Remember, the journey is the reward. So let's begin.

CHAPTER ONE

INTRODUCTION.

<u>introduction of the book</u>

Did school teach you how to control? Yeah, I am asking you that only did school teach you?

Wait! Wait! Wait! But what controlling? Which controlling? Do you think controlling means controlling which your school teacher denied you to go to the washroom and you controlled to stay in that situation? No. What do you think after seeing the book title? ''DO IT, DON'T DELAY.''

Let me explain to you what it mean.

We weren't thought some important skills in our schooling time, and we just listen to success stories and we think of to do that, this, and some other things. Here I'm not saying that the subjects you read like Physics, Social, Hindi, Biology and some, etc are a time waste of studying, these are necessary as well as we have to learn some basic skills which will help you to grow.

Your school taught you how to run in the race, but it didn't teach you how to win.

In the same manner, you learnt some subjects in school, but you didn't learn what is needed. And that's what this book is for. This book will almost cover all the topics in my view and different people's views. This book is written based on my experience, people's experience, interviews, and on public opinion.

When I was a student of 9th at that time, I used to have a book containing answers to the last 3 years question paper. That book helped me to understand the question paper pattern and some questions were repeated in my final exams.

In the same way, we have many questions in our daily life which we feel hard to ask in our school and later on, you won't be able to ask the same question because we think that " aree if I ask that question what will the teacher think? If I ask then my classmates will laugh at me?" by this mindset, we don't ask the question and that question changes into fear. In this book you will get the answer of the questions and you will learn skills from it, to make it easier I have made small content and high-quality knowledge which it will be very easier to understand and you will be mastering in it. But you have to implement it after reading each subtopic as there are some topics which contains some exercises and activities which you have to definitely follow it time to time to get better experience of this book. That's what the meaning the " DO IT, DON'T DELAY". Do and follow this book for better understanding and for better results, don't delay

This isn't just a book that will help and inspire you- it will visibly improve the way you live.

If by chance if you don't get enough knowledge or if you think this book is just useless after reading then you just can contact my team by doing DM to my Instagram Handle. In 24hrs you will getting full refund to your source of payment.

But I can give you the guarantee that you will definitely like this book and you will start enjoying this.

That's it of the introduction,

Thank you, I Hope You Enjoy This Book.

CHAPTER TWO

PUBLIC SPEAKING

Speaking in public can be a nerve-wracking experience for many people. Whether it's a business presentation, a speech at a wedding, or a talk at a conference, the thought of standing in front of a crowd and delivering a message can be daunting. However, with the right preparation and mindset, anyone can become a confident and effective public speaker. In this chapter, we'll explore some tips and techniques to help you speak in public with confidence and impact.

Know your audience.

One of the most important factors in successful public speaking is understanding your audience. What are their interests, concerns, and expectations? Tailor your message to meet their needs, and speak in a way that resonates with them. For example, if you're speaking to a group of professionals, use industry-specific jargon and data to support your points. If you're speaking to a general audience, use stories, humor, and everyday examples to make your message relatable and engaging.

Prepare and rehearse.

The more prepared you are, the more confident you'll feel when speaking in public. Take the time to research your topic, organize your thoughts, and create an outline or script. Rehearse your speech or presentation, either alone or in front of a trusted friend or family member, to refine your delivery and ensure that your message is clear and effective. Practice your tone of voice, your body language, and your eye contact, as these elements can greatly impact the way your message is received.

Engage your audience.

Engaging your audience is a key component of successful public speaking. Make eye contact, use gestures and movement to emphasize your points, and ask questions or invite feedback to involve your audience in the conversation. Use visual aids, such as slides or props, to illustrate your points and capture your audience's attention. Be mindful of your tone of voice and pacing, as these elements can greatly impact the way your message is received.

Be authentic.

One of the most effective ways to connect with your audience is to be authentic and genuine. Speak from the heart, and share personal anecdotes or experiences that illustrate your points. Be yourself, and don't try to emulate someone else's speaking style or personality. Authenticity and vulnerability can help to build trust and rapport with your audience, and make your message more memorable and impactful.

Manage your nerves.

It's natural to feel nervous when speaking in public, but there are techniques you can use to manage your nerves and perform at your best. Take deep breaths, practice visualization or meditation, and use positive self-talk to calm your mind and body. Focus on the message you want to deliver, and remember that your audience is rooting for you. Don't let nerves prevent you from sharing your message and making a positive impact.

In conclusion, speaking in public can be a powerful tool for communicating your ideas, building your brand, and inspiring others. By following these tips and techniques, you can become a confident and effective public speaker, and make a lasting impression on your audience. Remember to prepare, engage your audience, be authentic, and manage your nerves, and you'll be well on your way to delivering a successful and impactful speech or presentation.

CHAPTER THREE

HOW TO BE MY OWN BEST-FRIEND?

Be Your Own Best Friend

When life gets tough, it's easy to turn to others for support and guidance. However, sometimes we need to be our own best friends and provide ourselves with the love, care, and encouragement we need to thrive. In this chapter, we'll explore some tips and techniques for being your own best friend and cultivating a healthy, supportive relationship with yourself.

Practice self-compassion.

Self-compassion is the practice of treating ourselves with kindness, understanding, and acceptance. Instead of beating ourselves up for our flaws, mistakes, or setbacks, we can offer ourselves the same kindness and understanding we would offer to a dear friend. When we practice self-compassion, we give ourselves permission to be imperfect, and we cultivate a sense of empathy and connection with ourselves.

Set healthy boundaries.

Being your own best friend also means setting healthy boundaries and treating yourself with respect. This might mean saying no to requests or demands that don't align with your values or priorities, or speaking up for yourself when someone crosses a boundary. By setting healthy boundaries, you communicate to yourself that your needs and well-being matter and you protect yourself from unnecessary stress or harm.

Celebrate your successes.

As your own best friend, it's important to celebrate your successes and acknowledge your accomplishments. Whether it's a small win or a major achievement, take the time to pat yourself on the back and savor the moment. Celebrating your successes can boost your confidence, increase your motivation, and remind you of your worth and capabilities.

Practice self-care.

Self-care is the practice of taking care of our physical, emotional, and mental well-being. As your own best friend, it's important to prioritize self-care and give yourself the care and attention you need to thrive. This might include taking a relaxing bath, going for a walk in nature, or engaging in a creative hobby. Whatever self-care means to you, make it a priority in your life, and treat yourself with the love and care you deserve.

Cultivate a growth mindset.

A growth mindset is a belief that our abilities, talents, and intelligence can be developed through hard work, practice, and dedication. As your own best friend, cultivate a growth mindset by embracing challenges, seeking out new experiences, and learning from your mistakes. This mindset can help you overcome obstacles, build resilience, and reach your full potential.

In conclusion, being your own best friend is about cultivating a healthy, supportive relationship with yourself. By practicing self-compassion, setting healthy boundaries, celebrating your successes, practicing self-care, and cultivating a growth mindset, you can become your own biggest ally and supporter. Remember, you are the only person who will be with you for your entire life, so treat yourself with the love, kindness, and care you deserve.

Practice positive self-talk.

One of the easiest and most effective ways to be your own best friend is by practicing positive self-talk. This means replacing negative self-talk (such as "I'm not good enough" or "I can't do this") with positive, encouraging thoughts (such as "I am capable" or "I can handle this"). By reframing negative thoughts and replacing them with positive ones, we can boost our confidence, motivation, and self-esteem.

Embrace your uniqueness.

As your own best friend, it's important to embrace your uniqueness and individuality. This means accepting your quirks, flaws, and idiosyncrasies, and celebrating what makes you different from others. By embracing our uniqueness, we can cultivate a sense of self-acceptance and authenticity, and avoid the trap of comparison or self-judgment.

Create a self-care routine.

Self-care is an essential component of being your own best friend. By creating a self-care routine that includes activities that nourish your mind, body, and soul, you can prioritize your well-being and show yourself the care and attention you deserve. This might include activities such as meditation, yoga, journaling, reading, or spending time with loved ones.

Set realistic expectations.

When we set unrealistic expectations for ourselves, we set ourselves up for disappointment and self-judgment. As your own best friend, it's important to set realistic expectations for yourself and acknowledge that you are human and capable of making mistakes. By setting realistic expectations, we can avoid the pressure to be perfect and focus on progress rather than perfection.

Practice forgiveness.

As your own best friend, it's important to practice forgiveness, both towards yourself and others. This means letting go of grudges, resentment, and bitterness, and instead cultivating a sense of compassion and understanding. By practicing forgiveness, we can release ourselves from the burden of negative emotions and cultivate a sense of peace and inner harmony.

By incorporating these tips and strategies into yourife, you can become your own best friend and cultivate a healthy, supportive relationship with yourself. Remember, being your own best friend is a journey, not a destination. It requires patience, compassion, and a commitment to self-improvement. But with persistence and dedication, you can become your own biggest ally and supporter, and unlock your true potential.

CHAPTER FOUR

HOW CAN I ADD MEDITATION TO MY LIFESTYLE?

Adding meditation to your lifestyle can be a great way to reduce stress, increase mindfulness, and improve your overall well-being. Here are some steps and tips to help you incorporate meditation into your daily routine:

Choose a time and place: Select a time and place that will allow you to meditate without distractions. Find a quiet space where you can sit or lie down comfortably, and choose a time of day that works best for you. Many people find it helpful to meditate first thing in the morning or before bed.

Start small: If you're new to meditation, start with just a few minutes each day and gradually work your way up to longer sessions. Even just a few minutes of meditation each day can have a positive impact on your well-being.

Find a technique that works for you: There are many different types of meditation, so experiment with different techniques to find one that resonates with you. Some popular techniques include mindfulness meditation, loving-kindness meditation, and body scan meditation.

Set an intention: Before you begin your meditation practice, set an intention for what you hope to achieve or experience during your session. This can help you stay focused and present during your meditation.

Focus on your breath: Many meditation techniques involve focusing on the breath. To do this, simply observe your breath as it moves in and out of your body. When your mind begins to wander, gently bring your attention back to your breath.

Practice regularly: Consistency is key when it comes to meditation. Try to practice every day, even if it's just for a few minutes. Over time, you'll begin to notice the benefits of your practice.

Be patient: Meditation can be challenging, especially at first. It's normal to experience thoughts, emotions, and physical sensations during your meditation. Rather than getting frustrated or discouraged, try to approach your practice with curiosity and openness.

Seek support: If you're struggling with your meditation practice, consider seeking out a meditation teacher or joining a meditation group. This can provide you with guidance and support as you continue to develop your practice.

Remember, meditation is a practice, and it takes time and dedication to develop. With patience and persistence, however, you can incorporate this powerful tool into your daily routine and experience the many benefits it has to offer.

Use guided meditations: If you're having trouble focusing on your breath or quieting your mind, try using guided meditation. There are many apps and online resources that offer free guided meditations, which can help you stay focused and present during your practice.

Create a ritual: To help make meditation a habit, create a ritual around your practice. This could include lighting a candle, setting an intention, or playing calming music before you begin your meditation.

Practice in different locations: To keep your practice fresh and interesting, try meditating in different locations. You could try meditating outside in nature, in a yoga studio, or even in a different room in your home.

Set a timer: If you're new to meditation, it can be helpful to set a timer for your practice. This can help you stay focused and prevent you from getting distracted by thoughts of how much time has passed.

Be kind to yourself: It's important to approach your meditation practice with kindness and self-compassion. Don't judge yourself if you're finding it difficult to focus or if you're experiencing uncomfortable thoughts or emotions. Instead, simply observe these experiences and bring your attention back to your breath.

Make it a priority: If you're serious about incorporating meditation into your lifestyle, make it a priority. Schedule your practice into your calendar and treat it as you would any other important appointment.

Remember, meditation is a personal practice, and what works for one person may not work for another. Experiment with different techniques and strategies to find what resonates with you, and don't be afraid to ask for support or guidance if you need it. With patience and persistence, you can develop a regular meditation practice that supports your overall health and well-being.

CHAPTER FIVE

HABIT

For the longest time, I have been a student of habits.
I don't set goals, for two reasons:
– You do it for a destination, instead of becoming someone in the process
– You invariably start chasing another destination, upon reaching one.
Instead, habits have come to help me in the smallest to biggest things in life.
Be it a habit of sleeping on time.

I love habits because the kind of person I become pursuing them opens up multiple doors, instead of chasing goals that may (perhaps)
lead to just one door if one gets lucky.
Habits build us, goals lay us barren.

The trick to waking up early is not waking up early.
It is sleeping on time!
The secret is not merely waking up early. Any alarm clock could do that for you.

The secret is to be energized, happy, and productive in the morning.
Nothing could ensure this other than sleeping on time.
Otherwise, what's the use of waking up early and feeling groggy and eventually hating yourself?
Waking up early fizzles out, and sleeping on time is what flourishes.

Share your journey.
Document your journey.
Narrate your journey.

Why not?

The key to having more opportunities in life is to give yourself enough

opportunities to get curious.

You have no idea how the dumb questions that you avoid asking could

solve someone's dilemma that they can't avoid!

Targets are the enemy of habits.

Don't set targets.
Set habits!

Setting targets instead of habits makes us forget the kind of person

we want to become.

We not only want to run a marathon. We also want to get fit.

We not only want to look sculpted. We want to see how disciplined we are.

We do not want to crack just the sales numbers. We want to solve more customer problems.

The more we get the process right, the closer we get to the targets.

The more we run after targets, the more we sign up for feeling hollow

once we achieve them.

Habits hire us forever and take us higher, whereas targets tame us and leave us clueless after we achieve them.

Don't try to minimize your struggle.

Try to make it more meaningful.

You can never minimize your struggle. It will only suppress your emotions.

However, you can always figure out what it means.

Most important skill today that is hardly taught: Is self- Growth Business Development Health.

You won't get out of laziness for something you don't want to do.

I wake up at 4:30 a.m. every morning. After meditating, singing practice and reading.

Whether it is 36 degrees in June or 6 degrees in December. Just because I love it!

However, I might not do that to watch cricket on TV. Or I might not want to watch a trending series.

Only because I don't want to!

We don't need more productivity hacks. We need to spend more time

with ourselves doing what we want to do.

The best form of writing is the one that is written neither out of fear nor with the willingness to share.

Write not because you want to be liked.

Write not because you want more likes. Write not because someone else will be impressed by you.

Write, because you want to express yourself.

Write, because you will read it.

Write, because if you won't, your bottled-up emotions will harm you

alone.

Write, because if you won't write it, how will you ever read what you

need?

Write, because no one could ever be You 2.0.

To start the habit of reading books, read books that you will enjoy. Not books that the world thinks you should be reading! Three things that will tell you who/what you consider as

important in your life.

1. Your first hour after you wake up

2. Your last hour before you sleep

3. Your Calendar.

The first 60 minutes of my day are me-time.

I sip water like wine. Just smile at the blessings I have. Meditate.

The last 60 minutes of my day are family time.

The things that are easy to do are also the things that are easy to ignore.

If you choose to do them with consistency instead of ignorance, they

can change your life completely.

Daily progress isn't about becoming an expert in your field.

It is developing the mindset that progress is a way of life.

It is like breathing.

We rarely stop to acknowledge it.

But we breathe every second.

We would die without it.

Reading books will not make you smart.

Watching motivational videos will not make you driven. Writing will not make your thoughts clearer.

We are not shaped by these things.

We are shaped by the stories we tell ourselves.

Reading books isn't the answer. The answer is what we take away

from them.

Writing isn't the answer to clarity. The answer lies in whether we write to get more at peace or whether we write to seek validation.

Motivational videos certainly aren't the answer (even though I make a

bunch every week). The video we turn our life into after watching those videos is the answer.

Nothing changes until we change what lives between our two ears.

We know others through their actions.

We know ourselves through our thoughts.

What others are thinking, we don't know. We only know what they are doing.

That is exactly what they see when they look at us – what we do, instead of what we think.

We may have a hundred plans, but, what others see is the one we are executing.

Plans are plain without performance.

Thoughts are powerful when they are converted into actions.

Without action, they have simply broken promises.

We nod to show that we are listening.

But we are not listening to the opposite person.

Instead, we are listening to our minds telling us what to say.

When we listen, do we truly listen or are we preparing a response in

our heads?

When we listen, are we coming with an open mind, or just a closed

a book that knows all the answers?

When we listen, do we intend to help, or do we just want to impose our point of view?

We nod to show we are listening to respond.

However, what if we nodded to purely listen to what others have to truly convey?

What if we nodded to understand what was coming in, instead of structuring what we had already planned?

Your attendance doesn't define your discipline.

Your attention does.

College requires you to have certain attendance.

Some companies want you to be in the office for attendance.

Worse, even relatives want you to be present at parties you hate!

What if you are present, but not happily present?

You'll be lost, hating everyone, and hating your life.

Your discipline is defined when you are fully present, for all the times

you are present.

That shows you are interested, enjoying the process, and in the flow!

The quality of your presence is way more important than the forced
quantity of your attendance when you're not present.
Who you spend time with will define the stories you hear.
The stories you hear will define the stories in your head.
The stories in your head will define you.
    Optimize for learning, not salary.
Optimize for progress, not stability.
Optimize for facing fears, not for comfort.

If you have two job offers with a similar salary, the one with growth
is
the one you want to pick up.
If you want stability in terms of money and career, no one gets
it unless they embrace progress as their way of life.
Comfort stems from facing what you fear. Staying in the comfort
zone
is the most dangerous thing to do.

The things that are the easiest to do are the things that are the
hardest to live with.
Yet they are the only things that make our life easier.
    As a fresher, you do not have hope in hell of getting noticed.
Just work, don't ask questions, don't challenge, say yes to your boss,
and don't try to be too friendly.
The key is to stick around.
And lie low.
Just one of the many lies told to us.
Some of the smartest people in the world are competing for
your sleep time.
Do you know what that means?
Your sleep is VERY IMPORTANT!
to you AND them.
Don't let them win!
The social media and streaming platforms are designed in a manner
that hooks your attention.

The more you like the content
More they will recommend it.
More watch time. Less sleep time.
Disconnection helps, because motivation can't, especially if all the
smartest minds in the world are 24x7 thinking on how to keep you
glued.
Saying no to everything else and sleeping on time – are the greatest
the secret sauce of self-love.
Do not allow comfort to make you believe that you no longer
need to try!
You've got a good job through hard work.
Shouldn't try to get better anymore.
Having beautiful relationships with people you care for.
Shouldn't try to care for them anymore.
Got a sculpted body after relentless hard work.
Shouldn't try to maintain it anymore.
Wrong.
Comfort is a destination.
Trying more is a path.
To get to the next level of destination of comfort.
If we stay stuck in just one destination (comfort), we forget our
home
(happiness).
Happiness certainly never comes through staying cool in what
seems
comfortable.
Happiness is simply a result of slaying your comfort, so you always
stay comfortable staying out of your comfort zone.
No step is small, as long as it is headed in the direction of where we
want to go.
In a society that is obsessed with hard work and career
success, seeking boredom is an act of rebellion.
Seeking boredom through free time helps you feel comfortable in
your
skin.

Seeking boredom in your own company makes you not crave for anyone else's company.

Seeking boredom in the relentless daily habits makes you create success automatically.

We want success and work hard to get there, hardly ever knowing that the hardest work is to seek ease in the mundane.

Find it hard to say no to people, when you know you should?

It's mostly because you worry about what they will think of you.

If you follow the right set of people on social media,

opportunities will come by design.

Not by luck!

You become like the people you spend your time with – online and offline.

Approaching life questions.

Complaining or figuring out solutions.

Saying no to new things or asking 'what if's and 'why not'.

They are a result of the choices we've made to follow people online.

And it's almost impossible to not have great opportunities because following the right people teaches you how to create your life around

having new opportunities.

A sneak peek into my habits

While you now know what I think about habits, here is how habits think through me.

A sneak peeks, into my habits.

Habit 1

I always carry a notebook with me.

I take notes. I put tasks in a calendar.

I send myself emails in the future.

My mind's energy should be spent on thinking.

Not remembering!

Habit 2

Document EVERYTHING!

At any point, I have three notebooks
1. Ideas.
2. To-do lists for the day.
3. Meeting notes.
And I write things down.
Writing helps tell the brain that this is important.
And it helps me not to 'try and remember' anything.

Habit 3
I put everything on a calendar.
My calendar is my lifeline.
Everything is on my calendar.
Bills to pay, birthdays to remember, threads to write, weekly routines.
Over fifty percent of my waking time goes towards things that are important, but not urgent! :)

Habit 4
I schedule emails to myself, for the future.
There are so many things that interest me, that it becomes important
to prioritize.
And for me, prioritization is about scheduling.
Future emails serve that purpose.

Habit 5
Using technology for everything possible.
There are a lot of tasks that suck your time but do not make you move forward.
Consider using technology to solve them for you.
Habit 6
I have two WhatsApp self-groups.
Create a group on WhatsApp with someone.
Once done, delete that someone else.
Now it's just you in the group.

Pin that group to the top.
And use it for easy sharing and access.
1. Docs/Images
Which is where I store my important images (PAN Card, License
Copy, passport copy, etc.) and documents for easy access (tickets,
etc.).
2. Thoughts
Which I use to just type something on the run, or click something,
or
record/shoot something.

Habit 7
An afternoon nap is my daily ritual.
I grew up in a home where Ma insisted, we sleep for an hour after
lunch.
I guess that's just stayed.
Then I remember going to China and Korea and seeing that in
offices,
too, there was a culture of an afternoon nap (heads down on the
table)
I used to grab 15 minutes of a power nap while in school. Nothing
feels better :)

Habit 8
Setting the right environment is super important.
I never work from my bed, always on a table.
I never read lying down, always on a chair.
I never eat while watching something.
I never work in a dark room. Always natural light.
Even when it is work from home, change into 'office attire' while
working and not be in your PJs – subconsciously tricks your mind
to
get into the comfort zone!
Do not underestimate your surroundings while trying to create
flow!

The human mind is conditioned to feel happy and fulfilled while making
progress.
Set your life in such a manner that you can measure this progress.
Even a tiny improvement in your productivity will yield results over
time.

CHAPTER SIX

READING BOOK

Building a habit of reading can be a great way to improve your knowledge, enhance your creativity, and reduce stress. However, many people struggle to make reading a regular part of their lives. In this chapter, we'll explore some strategies for building a reading habit that sticks.

Set a Goal: To start building a reading habit, set a goal for how much you want to read. Start small – maybe just 10 minutes a day – and gradually increase the amount of time you spend reading each day. You can also set a goal for the number of books you want to read in a year. Having a specific goal can help keep you motivated and on track.

Choose Your Reading Material Carefully: If you're not enjoying the books you're reading, it will be harder to stick to your reading habit. Be intentional about the books you choose to read. Look for books that align with your interests, challenge you intellectually, or simply bring you joy. Consider asking for book recommendations from friends or using online resources to find books that pique your interest.

Create a Reading List: Creating a reading list is a great way to keep track of the books you want to read and stay motivated. Keep a list of books you want to read and refer to it when it's time to choose your next read.

Set a Specific Time for Reading: It can be helpful to establish a specific time for reading each day. Choose a time when you're most alert and focused – for many people, this is in the morning or at night. Make reading a part of your daily routine, just like brushing your teeth or exercising.

Make Reading Convenient: Keep your reading material in a place where it's easy to access. This could be a bookshelf in your bedroom, a stack of books on your coffee table, or an e-reader that's always within reach. The easier it is to pick up a book and start reading, the more likely you are to stick to your reading habit.

Minimize Distractions: When it's time to read, try to eliminate distractions as much as possible. Turn off your phone, find a quiet space, and focus your attention on your book. This will help you get into the flow of reading and stay engaged in the story.

Join a Reading Group: Joining a book club or reading group can be a great way to stay motivated and make reading a social activity. Not only will you have people to discuss your reading material with, but you'll also be held accountable for finishing the book on time.

Track Your Progress: Keeping track of your reading progress can be a great way to stay motivated. Set up a reading log or use an app to track the number of books you've read and the amount of time you've spent reading. Celebrate your accomplishments along the way to keep your motivation high.

In summary, building a habit of reading takes time and effort, but the benefits are well worth it. Choose your reading material carefully, set a goal, create a reading list, make reading convenient, and minimize distractions. With patience and persistence, you can build a reading habit that brings joy, inspiration, and knowledge to your life.

Mix Up Your Reading Material: To keep things interesting, try mixing up the types of books you read. For example, you could alternate between fiction and non-fiction, or switch between different genres. This will help keep your reading habit fresh and prevent you from getting bored.

Find a Reading Buddy: Having someone to discuss your reading material with can be a great motivator. Find a friend or family member who shares your interest in reading, and make a commitment to discuss the books you read together. This will keep you accountable and help you stay engaged in your reading habit.

Read in Different Formats: Don't limit yourself to just one type of reading material. Consider reading physical books, e-books, audiobooks, and even magazines or newspapers. This will help you stay engaged in your reading habit and give you more flexibility in how and where you read.

Make Reading a Priority: To build a habit of reading, you need to make it a priority in your life. This means setting aside time for reading each day and making it a non-negotiable part of your routine. Treat reading like any other important activity in your life, and you'll be more likely to stick to your habit.

Make Reading Enjoyable: Finally, it's important to make reading an enjoyable experience. This means finding a comfortable spot to read, setting the right mood with lighting and music, and choosing books that you genuinely enjoy. When you make reading a pleasurable experience, you'll be more likely to look forward to it each day and stick to your reading habit in the long term.

Remember, building a reading habit takes time and effort, but it's well worth it. Reading can help you expand your knowledge, improve your cognitive function, and reduce stress. With patience, persistence, and a few tips and tricks, you can make reading a regular part of your life.

CHAPTER SEVEN

PROCRASTINATION

Procrastination is a common behavior that affects many people in various aspects of their lives. It can have negative consequences on your productivity, health, and overall well-being. However, by understanding the root causes of procrastination and implementing effective strategies, you can overcome procrastination and achieve your goals. In this essay, we will explore some tips and tricks to help you avoid procrastination.

Understand the Root Causes of Procrastination Procrastination is often caused by underlying emotional and psychological factors, such as anxiety, perfectionism, and fear of failure. These factors can make it difficult to start or complete a task, causing you to delay it or avoid it altogether. By understanding your personal triggers for procrastination, you can start to work through these issues and develop a plan to address them.

Break Down Tasks into Smaller Steps One of the most effective ways to overcome procrastination is to break down larger tasks into smaller, more manageable steps. This approach can help you avoid feeling overwhelmed and make it easier to get started on a task. You can also set specific deadlines for each step to keep yourself accountable and on track.

Use Positive Self-Talk and Visualization Negative self-talk can be a major barrier to productivity and can lead to procrastination. To combat this, try using positive self-talk and visualization techniques to motivate yourself. Remind yourself of the benefits of completing a task and visualize yourself successfully completing it. This can help boost your confidence and motivation, making it easier to get started on a task.

Prioritize Your Tasks Another effective strategy for avoiding procrastination is to prioritize your tasks. Identify the tasks that are most important and urgent, and focus your energy on completing them first. This can help prevent you from getting bogged down by less important tasks and can also give you a sense of accomplishment as you complete each task.

Eliminate Distractions Distractions can be a major roadblock to productivity and can lead to procrastination. To avoid distractions, try eliminating them as much as possible. This might mean turning off your phone or social media notifications while you work or finding a quiet, distraction-free workspace. When you minimize distractions, you can focus your energy and attention on the task at hand.

Use Time-Management Strategies Time-management strategies can be an effective tool for avoiding procrastination. Set specific, realistic goals for each day or week, and create a schedule to help you stay on track. Use tools like calendars and to-do lists to keep yourself organized and accountable.

Additionally, consider using a timer or tracking tool to help you stay focused and on task.

Take Breaks and Practice Self-Care Taking breaks and practicing self-care can also help you avoid procrastination. When you take regular breaks, you can prevent burnout and stay focused on your tasks. Additionally, make time for activities that you enjoy, such as exercise or hobbies, to help reduce stress and improve your overall well-being. When you take care of yourself, you'll be better equipped to tackle tasks and avoid procrastination.

In conclusion, procrastination can be a challenging behavior to overcome, but by understanding the root causes of procrastination and implementing effective strategies, you can improve your productivity and achieve your goals. By breaking down tasks into smaller steps, using positive self-talk and visualization, prioritizing tasks, eliminating distractions, using time-management strategies, and practicing self-care, you can overcome procrastination and become a more productive and successful person. Remember, it takes time and effort to break a habit of procrastination, but with patience and persistence, you can achieve great results.

CHAPTER EIGHT

TIME MANAGEMENT

Introduction to Time Management

Effective time management is essential for achieving your goals and getting things done. Time is a finite resource, so it is crucial to use it wisely. In this chapter, we'll explore the basics of time management and how to get started.

The first step to effective time management is to set clear goals. By identifying what you want to achieve, you can plan your time and prioritize the most important tasks. Once you have set your goals, it's time to create a schedule. Your schedule should be tailored to your needs and preferences, and it should include time for work, rest, and leisure.

One of the keys to successful time management is to be realistic about how long tasks will take. Overestimating or underestimating the time required can lead to frustration, stress, and missed deadlines. It's important to set aside enough time for each task and to avoid multitasking, which can reduce productivity and increase stress.

Another critical aspect of time management is to identify and minimize time-wasters. These can include social media, email, and other distractions that can eat up your time. It's important to set boundaries and limit your exposure to these distractions during times when you need to focus on your work.

Finally, it's essential to take breaks and allow yourself time to recharge. Taking regular breaks can improve productivity and reduce fatigue, helping you to be more focused and efficient in the long run.

By implementing these strategies, you can begin to improve your time management skills and make the most of your precious time.

Time management is about making the most of the time you have to achieve your goals. But to effectively manage your time, you must first set clear goals and priorities. This chapter will guide you through the process of setting goals and prioritizing your tasks.

The first step in effective goal setting is to identify what you want to achieve. Whether it's a short-term or long-term goal, you need to be specific about what you want to accomplish. Make sure your goals are realistic and achievable and don't be afraid to break them down into smaller, more manageable steps.

Once you have identified your goals, it's time to prioritize your tasks. Not all tasks are created equal, and some are more important than others. Start by making a list of all the tasks you need to accomplish, and then assign a priority level to each one.

To help with prioritization, you can use the Eisenhower Matrix, a simple tool that helps you categorize tasks based on their level of urgency and importance. Tasks that are urgent and important should be tackled first, while tasks that are less urgent and less important can be delegated or delayed.

In addition to setting goals and prioritizing tasks, it's essential to have a plan for achieving your goals. This can include creating a timeline for completing tasks, breaking down larger projects into smaller tasks, and setting deadlines to help you stay on track.

By setting clear goals and priorities and having a plan for achieving them, you can manage your time more effectively and achieve the results you desire.

Once you have identified your goals and priorities and have a plan for achieving them, it's time to start tracking and analyzing your time. This chapter will guide you through the process of tracking your time and analyzing how you spend it.

The first step in time tracking is to create a time log. This can be done using a simple spreadsheet or a specialized app designed for time tracking. In your time log, you should record all the activities you do throughout the day, including work tasks, leisure activities, and personal tasks.

Once you have a time log, it's time to analyze how you spend your time. Start by looking for patterns and trends in your time log. Are there activities that take up a lot of your time but don't contribute to your goals or priorities? Are there times of the day when you are most productive, or times when you tend to procrastinate?

Use this information to make changes to your time management habits. For example, if you find that you are spending too much time on social media, you can set limits on your screen time or use tools to block distracting websites during work hours. If you find that you are most productive in the morning, you can schedule your most important tasks for that time.

In addition to analyzing your time log, it's also essential to take regular breaks and practice good time management habits. Make sure to take breaks throughout the day to refresh your mind and body, and use techniques like the Pomodoro Technique to stay focused and productive.

By tracking and analyzing your time, you can identify areas where you are wasting time and make changes to improve your productivity and achieve your goals. Remember, time is your most valuable resource, so use it wisely!

As you work to manage your time and achieve your goals, you may find that there are tasks that you simply don't have the time or skills to complete on your own. In these cases, delegating or outsourcing tasks can be a powerful tool for improving your time management and increasing your productivity.

Delegating tasks involves assigning tasks to others who are better equipped to handle them. This could mean assigning tasks to coworkers, employees, or even family members. When delegating, it's important to choose the right person for the job and provide clear instructions on what needs to be done.

Outsourcing tasks involves hiring a third party to complete tasks for you. This could mean hiring a virtual assistant, a freelancer, or a specialized company. Outsourcing can be particularly useful for tasks that require specialized skills or knowledge, such as graphic design or software development.

Delegating and outsourcing can be an effective way to free up time and focus on the tasks that are most important to you. However, it's important to remember that delegating and outsourcing do require an investment of time and money, so it's essential to weigh the costs and benefits before deciding to delegate or outsource a task.

In addition to delegating and outsourcing, it's also important to learn how to say no to tasks that aren't a priority or that you simply don't have the time to complete. Saying no can be difficult, but it's an important skill for effective time management.

By delegating, outsourcing, and saying no when necessary, you can free up time and focus on the tasks that are most important to you. This can help you achieve your goals and improve your productivity in both your personal and professional life.

CHAPTER NINE

COMMUNICATION SKILLS

Effective communication is the cornerstone of success in every area of life. Whether you're building relationships, advancing your career, or pursuing personal goals, the ability to communicate clearly, confidently, and authentically is essential. In this chapter, we'll explore some strategies for developing your communication skills and overcoming common obstacles to effective communication.

Cultivate Active Listening

One of the most important aspects of effective communication is active listening. When we truly listen to others, we demonstrate respect, empathy, and openness, which helps to create a positive and productive communication environment. To become a better listener, try the following:

Pay attention to nonverbal cues like body language, facial expressions, and tone of voice.

Avoid interrupting or formulating a response before the other person has finished speaking.

Practice empathy by putting yourself in the other person's shoes and considering their perspective.

Develop Clarity and Confidence

To communicate effectively, it's important to be clear and confident in your message. This means being able to articulate your thoughts and ideas in a way that others can understand and relate to. To develop clarity and confidence in your communication:

Practice organizing your thoughts and ideas before speaking.

Use clear and concise language to express your message.

Work on projecting confidence through body language and tone of voice.

Manage Your Emotions

Emotions can be a powerful force in communication, but they can also be a barrier to effective communication. To communicate effectively, it's important to learn how to manage your emotions and respond in a calm and rational manner. To manage your emotions:

Practice deep breathing and other relaxation techniques to reduce anxiety and stress.

Avoid reacting impulsively or emotionally to situations, instead, take a moment to consider your response.

Be aware of triggers that may cause emotional responses and develop strategies to manage them.

Build Rapport and Connection

Effective communication is not just about the message, it's also about building rapport and connection with others. To build rapport and connection:

Find common ground and use it as a starting point for conversation.

Demonstrate interest and curiosity in the other person's thoughts and ideas.

Practice active listening and empathy to establish a sense of mutual understanding.

By cultivating active listening, developing clarity and confidence, managing your emotions, and building rapport and connection, you can become a more effective communicator and unlock greater success in all areas of your life.

Use Open-Ended Questions

Open-ended questions are a great way to encourage conversation and demonstrate an interest in the other person's thoughts and ideas. By asking open-ended questions, you invite the other person to share more about themselves and their experiences. Some examples of open-ended questions include:

"What do you think about...?"

"Can you tell me more about...?"

"How did you feel when...?"

Practice Assertiveness

Being assertive is an important part of effective communication. Assertiveness means being able to express your needs and wants in a clear and respectful way, while also being open to the needs and wants of others. To practice assertiveness:

Use "I" statements to express how you feel and what you need.

Avoid blaming or criticizing others.

Be open to negotiation and compromise.

Learn to Give and Receive Feedback

Feedback is an essential part of growth and development, but it can be difficult to give and receive. To become more comfortable with feedback:

Practice giving constructive feedback in a respectful and non-judgmental way.

Be open to receiving feedback and use it as an opportunity to learn and grow.

Focus on specific behaviors or actions, rather than making generalizations or assumptions.

Practice, Practice, Practice

Like any skill, communication takes practice to master. Look for opportunities to practice your communication skills in everyday life, such as in conversations with friends and family, in professional settings, or even in public speaking. With practice, you'll become more confident, effective, and authentic in your communication.

By incorporating these tips into your communication toolkit, you can become a more effective and confident communicator, leading to greater success and fulfillment in all areas of your life.

CHAPTER TEN

HOW CAN I HAVE A SLEEP ROUTINE?

Why is sleep given so much importance?

I am young, I want to live life to the Max, sometimes not even sleep!

I have a friend called Jayanth. He usually sleeps till morning 11:00 AM, approximately he sleeps 12 to 14 hours, I don't understand why?

Go back to when you were a kid. As a robot, you have a fixed bedtime, eating time, playtime, etc.

As a kid growing up, you had the same school time, self-study at home, playtime, bedtime, etc.

What do you think those routines did to you as a kid?

I think so you hated those routines!

I understand. But what did they end up doing for you, though?

But you hated these routines right, at that time when you have to follow this routine you got the results.

Yes, you may have enjoyed it!

These days people enjoy the results more than the process.

No one loves

adhering to routines.

But everyone loves the

results routine bring.

The world is young. The world is shiny. The 'cool' world 'doesn't sleep'.

Expect that biologically we need sleep. Sleep that serves our mind and body the right way.

Be mindful though not to confuse randomness with spontaneity. Spontaneity leads to creativity, for which we must make room. However, not having a schedule, particularly a sleep schedule, is deceiving ourselves under the mask of productivity. Think of it like going to a park every evening once you are done with your work. You just go there without your phone, and you let yourself unwind. This is your routine. You are 100% certain to not come up with the same thoughts every day. They will be random. This is the spontaneity we scheduled for. By having a routine.

But when you don't have a routine, going to the park will be replaced with tasks not done and worries not solved.

Having a healthy sleep routine is the foundation of what you want to do for the rest of the day.

A healthy sleep routine starts with sleeping on time. Every single day of the week.

You plan your day. You fix your bedtime. And you stay true to it. Like clockwork. To tell our body that it is time. To respect its need to rest.

That makes a lot of sense. Can I tell you something, what if some days you are delayed due to work?

Such days, by design, should be few. Else they are consuming your day already!

Now answer my question:

What do you do in last 30-60 minutes before you go to bed?

I will only answer to your question, I know, I know: 45-50 mins Instagram. 1hr YouTube shorts/ or videos/ Netflix. Final 45-60 mins chatting {it may be friends, crush, girlfriend, boyfriend etc.}

That will make sure your sleep cycle is anything but fixed.

You should be sorry. To yourself. When you watch something that stimulates your senses, your body gets no signal that it is time to unwind. Instead, you are feeding it with emotions that spark even further emotions. Laughter leads to surprise leads to fear leads to sadness leads to sorrow.

The right approach is to not have contact with the screen at least 60 minutes before you go to your bed and after you wake-up. Keep your body calm.

But what will you do in these 60 minutes?

Anything that doesn't activate your senses. Reading books is a beautiful way. But the right books. Not thrillers. North fantasy. Perhaps poetry. A simple story. Or journaling. Or soft music that soothes you.

When you wake up in the morning wake up slowly.

We often wake up just in time for our day. Just in time for our classes, just in time for our bus, just in time for our meeting/call. Doing so leads to an imbalanced mind and body.

Wake up slowly. Drink water, read book, exercise, read affirmations, meditation or do something that will bring you to normal state.

The main point is you need to have productive, energetic, and good healthy sleep.

By chance if your friends plan a party tonight, you say no to them. If they force you, you please intimate them about your sleep routine. They may comment on you regarding this sleep routine, then you come to a conclusion that they are your toxic friends.

It is your life and it is your responsibility to keep your health healthy. Live for yourself not for your friends or parties or programs.

I know that your wise enough to understand this.

HOW CAN I PICK MYSELF UP.

As a kid, it was so easy to pick yourself up after a fall. As an adult, you struggle to do it.

The biggest reason you feel like a failure is that you are not sure whether you will ever get a shoot again at winning.

You feel like a failure because you are not sure of winning again.

This is sad but true. You do not need to get over it. You simply need to remind yourself that failing simply means failure in the journey. Not in the eventual outcome.

We feel like a failure because we think we cannot get to a point of winning again.

But they strain to think about winning is that it isn't about winning. It is about a feeling of progress.

Say you are playing a game of badminton with an opponent, and you are down by a score of 1 – 7. A friend passes by and asks for your score. You are embarrassed at that moment. You feel like a failure. Sheepishly you share the score. Your friend doesn't read too much into it and moves on after saying comforting words, 'don't worry, keep playing'. You eventually lose the match, but you lose it 8 – 10.

The same friend passes by and, out of courtesy, asks you for the score again. This time, though, is different. You are now filled with a sense of pride. You say you lost 8 – 10. What just happened here? You lost, and yet you felt good about yourself? You lost, and yet you moved from feeling like a failure to feeling like you want something.

How? This is so fascinating. So true. you would feel like a winner at that moment, even though you lost. Because you experienced progress. Because you realised you can win if you keep at it. Winning is not the purpose of life. To get better at living it is.

And this sense of progress is what will pick you up whenever you are down.

This is the symbol of progress, if you think that you are going to win after losing then you are inviting success into your life. If you bring even 1% more than before, so feel like a winner, because you are capable of doing anything.

But if your progress graph is going down instead of growing then you need to feel like a failure.

Pick up yourself every time by checking your progress from time to time.

By experience I am saying, no one checks how much hard work you did, people will appreciate your success.

If you fail, they will find your mistakes.

Don't sacrifice your dreams, just move on. Leave people behind. No one cares. Pickup yourself.

CHAPTER TWELVE

HOW DO I SAY NO?

Most frequently people don't say no, and except for everything. Saying yes for everything is too dangerous than failure. We have to learn how to say no in the right place. You feel very bad while saying no to others. Even though you want to say no with all your heart, 2X of your heart makes you feel bad about saying it. Why do you think it happens?

Let me say something with fully understanding and appreciating the context. You are worried to say no because you care what people may think of you. The reality is, a lot of us are raised in an environment were saying yes is a reflection off capability and saying no is a reflection of lack of intent.

Also, you worry that you would appear selfish or disrespectful to the person making the request. Again, it is about what you think people think of you. So how do you say no?

Here is what I do. **I seek permission to say no.**

Let's say you have been invited to a party, which you are not interested in that. Simply because you do not enjoy yourself there.

However, you think that saying no straight away might sound disrespectful. So, you ask: 'is it okay if say no?' **How do you think they are going to respond?**

Instead of saying no, ask if it's okay to say no? Fuel object to that.

When you ask this question, you are suddenly asking for permission instead of putting forward your imposition. And very few people would not grant that to you unless it is absolutely critical for you to say yes.

But why are so many of us so scared of drawing boundaries? We are scared of saying no in relationships, friendships offices or anywhere. How can you change the notion within yourself so that you don't feel guilty.

There are 2 parts to this. One is standing up for yourself. And 2, feeling guilty about it.

Let's start with the first part: standing up for yourself. My question to you is: if something is important to you, why can you not give it to the importance it deserves?

Why are you so conditioned into thinking that you cannot ask for your space? When was someone else's space important but not yours?

It's okay to put yourself first. It's absolutely okay to love yourself first because nothing flows out of an empty cup.

I just wish people will put this as a signboard on their bathroom mirrors so that they see it first thing in the morning.

My friend, do you know,

Most people are not aware of what you are going through?

They do not perceive the situation the same way that you do?

They need to be helped. They need to see what we are thinking. And that happens through a conversation. **Do not expect them to understand. You explain yourself.**

Why do you not want to go out with them?

Your answers: I am tired and if I go, I will only bring down the energy of the group. It is not that I do not love them or their company. But today is just a hard day.

Who's stopping you from seeing this to your friends? If you say no without having a conversation, it might feel like a rejection. However, you need to share what you truly feel with them.

I have been feeling very tired. I have not been feeling like myself. I know if I come along, I will not enjoy it, and I may end up spoiling everyone else mood as well. So, is it okay if I say no?

If they are the right friends, they will understand. However, if you are not understood, I would argue that they might not be worthy of you, and you are far better off not having friends than having those who want you to not be yourself in a conversation.

This makes it so clear.

And in saying no, there is no shame. Who knows, it might just help you to uncover your true relationships.

CHAPTER THIRTEEN

HOW DO I DEAL WITH TOXIC FRIENDS.

Sometimes, you may feel that one of your friends have turned toxic. But you don't know for sure. Is there a way to find out?

The reality, my friend, is no one becomes toxic on purpose. As much as people do not want to, some still end up becoming unhealthy for us. We all are attracted to people who do not have what we have. Not just in terms of physical possessions but personality traits as well. The early excitement of meeting someone new, getting to know them, forming a friendship all makes it really hard for us to know the true person inside.

That true person emerges in time. What started as a beautiful bond could transform into something undesirable.

This makes you very sad. Which is why we must understand that toxicity is an emotion. Not a source of truth. 2 people who are toxic for each other could very well be wonderful as individuals.

It is not always the person. It is the emotion that the relationship generates that makes the bond toxic. Any friendship that harms you- emotionally, mentally, psychologically- is he feeling you live through. That feeling should promote you to look into yourself and explore it.

What is that is disturbing me? What do I want to protect? Why is it such an important value to me? What part of me is it pointing towards?

The toxicity you feel in a relationship is an opportunity to understand your relationship with yourself.

This will lead you to an eventual question: what are these emotions trying to tell me about myself. Difficult situations do not test us, they reveal us. **Think of happiness.**

Let's say your value system is to be responsible for your happiness. If someone else holds your responsible for their happiness, the friendship becomes toxic. Until you don't know this fact about yourself, you will never realise what it is about the other person's behaviour that makes the relationship toxic.

Once you know what makes the friendship toxic, you heal it through conversation.

You sit and talk with them and honestly admit what you feel. An honest conversation with your friend on how this friendship is affecting you. **You do not complain. You do not accuse. You do not offer solutions. You simply share what you feel. And allow them to hear you out.**

The conversation will reveal a lot. About both of you. You will realize where they have to change.

What if they do not change? May be the other person does not want to change. Maybe you do not want to change.

Perhaps the conclusion is that what worked in the past may not work now.

And you decide to move on instead of holding on to something that is draining you both.

May be the other person does not want to change. Maybe you do not want to change. Then both of you start working towards reimagining the relationship.

It may not be easy, but it is what will liberate you eventually.

The truth in almost every friendship is that you are not able to see clearly watch this friendship can lead you into. However, whenever you figure out the not- so-good side of that friendship, the question is: what do you do about it?

We would all be wondering lonely if he walked away from all our friendships at the slightest difficulty. We can learn from this experience. We reflect on the traits of the other person that were always visible, but we choose to ignore. And it then becomes a responsibility to be aware of this in all future relationships. We learn from our mistakes.

Once you became aware of it. Then remind yourself of why you entered into this friendship in the first place. Because it made you happy. Because you wanted to be happy in it. So do everything that you need to do to be happy in it again. This simple yardstick solves everything- how can I make the relationship happy again?

Ask the question to yourself and answer it to yourself?

CHAPTER FOURTEEN

HOW DO I MAKE FRIENDS?

Isn't it so weird that as a kid you never struggled to make friends and now, as an adult, you find it so hard?

The best way to make friends is not to start by making friends in the first place. It is this argument to try to make friends that always makes us present a side of ours that is somewhat fake and pretentious. Our desperation also prevents us from seeing the other person properly or if there are any red flags in their personality.

The next thing we know, we find ourselves in a friendship that doesn't have a real version of ourselves, and we feel morally and emotionally obligated to continue that friendship.

Is that way why you continue being in that friendship despite it not working out for you?

Yes. We may have changed. It is possible we were never who the other person imagined us to be.

To build strong friendships, do not go out desperately looking for friends.

Your best friends are the ones who didn't even start with the intent of becoming friends with. You were simply being you. So were they. Because both of you let your guard down, you happen to see sites of each other without a façade. That authenticity led you to an awareness of what you liked or didn't like in each other. When there was significant overlap, you become friends.

For any relationship. Even a romantic one. Be interested in people. Genuinely interested in people. Ask them about their life, their interests, their experiences. Not to become their friend or to get them too like you. Instead, with a desire to know them. Authentically.

Be interested in people. Genuinely interested in people.

Especially in this digital world. there are so many examples of people who became friends on Twitter, Discord, Instagram, Facebook and etc., just by interacting with each other's content. Even before they knew it, they were friends without even meeting each other!

If and when you meet such friends in real life, their bond is so much stronger than most others would have, because the bond did not start with any expectation! Some of them may or may not turn into friends. Same may remain just connections. And that's okay too.

There are some people who think they do not need friends. There happy in their own company.

Here is the biggest truth of life- the only best friend you will ever have is yourself. You know who you are. Your deepest secrets. Your ability to talk yourself out of or into something.

How your stories have defined your existence more than anyone else.

There is no bigger joy than finding comfort in your own presence.

However, there is no bigger disservice to yourself when you use your shyness or social awkwardness or your unwillingness to be uncomfortable as a mask to not meet new people.

How do you know the difference between the two?

You already know it in your heart. You just have to be brutally honest with yourself. If you are honest, you really do not need anyone else. If you are not, then you are running away from yourself.

If you are at a point in life where you enjoy your own company, cool, continue enjoy it! If you are at a point in life where you think you need friends around, connect with people. They might not end up becoming friends, but even hanging out with people tells you so much about who you want and don't want to be.

And that is precious by itself.

I must say that having friends is actually wonderful because they allow you to meet a part of you that isn't a part of you. **The smile let your success.Lament at your loss.**

Even if you are friends are different from you which is true for many of us, the way they see the world differently helps you expand your definition of what the world is.

That is the magic of authenticity. Very few people can share those emotions while being completely honest. If you can do that to yourself, you are your best friend. If you want a friend to do that, that is as good as having an honest relationship with yourself.

All friendships boils down to being honest.

CHAPTER FIFTEEN

CONTROLLING YOUR-SELF

Introduction

These days we feel very hard to control ourselves and do whatever we think, we don't think that it is right or wrong. If we cannot control ourselves how can we control the second person. If we start controlling ourselves then we are unstoppable. There are some things that you have to start learning it knows itself, you are not supposed to delay or procrastinate it.

This chapter has 8 parts which have been taken into the consideration. These really help you and you will start seeing change in yourself if you start implementing what you learnt from each part or from each page of the book.

1. *HOW DO I DEVELOP PATIENCE?*

In these days people start doing something creative, they learn something new, or else they buy and start reading it but they won't complete it till the end. There are some people who are dedicated to their work and complete it to produce results. These people be like:

Pushpa Raj jhukega nahi; Thaggede le

The main point that we notice in people, not only you even me, I used to be like that but not right now. We start with 1000% power, energy, and with happiness, but we don't complete that work because of you don't have PATIENCE to complete it as you want knowledge in the half work. How many of you agree me? Everyone will agree because I was like that before.

Don't worry in further pages I will start giving you the solution for the question (1.1 HOW DO I DEVELOP PATIENCE?)

If you desire a more fulfilling relationship or a better working environment, you must learn how to develop patience and self-control. Patience is the ability to accept or tolerate delays, and problems without complaining.

In a world that has been programmed for so much hurry, a little patience when we deal with other people will help us to be sane.

I have a friend, so called Jayanth

This book may be slight boring but I am totally trying my best to make it funny and understandable.

Jayanth used to be one of the lazy guys in our 8th class and one of my best friends. One day another friend '' Aaryan '' who suggested a book for Jayanth. And he was ready to buy that book and he ordered that book on the online store.

I was surprised that ''from when this guy stared reading this book'' and the twist is till now he just completed reading 12-18 pages only as far I know. Later I understood that he doesn't want to wait till that book complete he was just waiting for results.

Your brain would be a total mess, you would have anger issues. And this would lead to stress and some physical and mental health complications.

Below are ten great suggestions for how to develop patience and self-control.

The key to everything is patience. You get the egg by hatching the egg, not by smashing it.

Arnold H Glasgow

1. Let your mind drift.

When we are focused so much on a particular thing and it doesn't go as planned, we tend to get impatient and lose self-control. For you to solve this problem

First, keep in mind that things don't always go as planned. Second, because something hasn't gone as planned doesn't mean it won't.

So, the next time you're in a store and the cashier seems to be taking forever, just let your thoughts wander. Distract yourself with your phone, or engage in a conversation. Anything, as long as it takes your mind from the current situation.

2. *Refuse to be in a hurry*

Impatience is often triggered by the internal and external pressure we feel. We get this nagging feeling that time is flying and we are missing out on something.

It's quite understandable if you feel this way. but as they say, too much hurry makes less haste.

You need a clear head to make good decisions. And panicking, losing self-control, and getting impatient never did anybody any right.

3. Think of all the times you got impatient

Consider all the times you have been impatient, and the nasty aftertaste it left. the remorse. The feelings of regret. I don't have any great memory of being impatient, if you do I promise they'll be very few.

The next time you want to snap, resist the urge. It's not necessary to always snap at people for them to perform their duties.

This bomb can be defused by recalling all the awful emotions you had while you were impatient. It's the equal of putting out a fire with a fire extinguisher.

4. *Be aware of your awareness*

When the Indian sage Atman Anda Krishna Menon was asked how to know when one is established in one's true nature, he is said to have replied, "When thoughts, feelings, sensations, and

perceptions can no longer take you away."
Rupert Spira

You are human, and you will become irritated if nothing changes. While some people can be more patient than others, everyone experiences impatience.

So, the next time you find yourself getting impatient again, try to be aware of that moment. Be an observer of your emotions, and just sit back and let things take the time they take. Breathe, focus your thought on your breathing, how it feels to breathe. You can also focus on your skin, the texture, and what a marvel it is.

5. Control every other feeling

Hardly do we ever feel only impatience. A lot of times there is anger and restlessness, and some sort of violence in our blood when we are impatient.

For you to develop patience and self-control you must be aware of them and also learn how to control them.

Count from 1 to 10 if you think you might lose your self-control. Counting from 1 to 10 might seem like one of those cliches we've always heard of but believe me it works. Take things very slowly.

Count from 1 to 10, while taking deep breaths between each count. Doing this distils whatever bad feeling you might have.

6. Think of all the reasons why you should wait

I think in order to accomplish anything in life, you have to visualize yourself there-accepting the award, hearing your song on the radio, whatever it is-or you lose the willpower and the drive.
Daya

If you're saving for a new device, and you feel you can no longer wait, visualize the phone and consider how much pleasure you'd get from holding it.

So is the same for everything. If you have something, a financial goal, or some business you are trying to build, think of the reward. The thought of this will fill you with the motivation and patience you need.

7. Stay silent or choose what you say

"Speak when you are angry and you will make the best speech you will ever regret."
Ambrose Bierce

Sometimes, speaking a single word is enough to send us spiralling down another episode of anger and impatience.

If you find yourself at the point where you've had enough and want to lose control, don't.

In situations where you cannot remain silent, take your time and chose your response. speaking slowly and quietly will also help you to have to regain patience and self-control.

I promise that people will listen to you better when you are calm and reasonable.

8. Get emotionally intelligent

Recognizing the source of your emotions is the first step toward emotional intelligence. Why are you impatient? Should you really be impatient?

Emotional intelligence is also noticing how your emotions affect those around you.

If you become frustrated, you can say hurtful things or do hurtful things to someone you care about.

Knowing that things don't always have to be about you will also help you develop some patience.

9. Relax

You have to give yourself time and the way you can do that is to relax and accept your weaknesses.

Life doesn't have to be gloom and doom all the time.

Start from the smallest place where your patience and self-control might be tested. Count those victories first before moving on to bigger things. This will give you the mindset you need to achieve other things you set your mind to.

Only by accepting that you really need to work on your patience will you truly begin to make progress.

Learning how to be more patient is difficult work, but once conquered, you will find life is easier.

Catherine Pulsifier.

10. *Take your time to do the work*

Developing patience and self-control is not for the faint of heart. But can you do it, yes, you can.

As humans we are bound to have feelings, sometimes these feelings are good, and at other times, they are less gracious. What feelings we have do not matter. What matters is how you control these feelings.

If you are somebody who has always acted on impulse, trying to develop patience and self-control might seem impossible, but it is quite easy to do.

All you have to do is to take it one step at a time. If you notice that you are always in a hurry when driving, slow down. If you notice that you can't wait for your savings to grow, you can, and they will if you just let them.

Patience is not the ability to wait, but the ability to keep a good attitude while waiting.

Why it is important that you learn how to develop patience and self-control

First, we need to be very patient and have some self-control for us to enjoy a healthy relationship with the people we love. While we may adore our partner and vice versa, they do have a knack for making us upset, but with patience, we can easily navigate through these situations.

You can only fail if you have no patience and self-control when starting out a business. The first few years always require the most patience. And lots of self-control when you begin to make the first profit.

Learning a musical instrument is impossible if you are impatient. This is because you will constantly have to fail and start again and fail and start again and fail and start again. Without patience and self-control, you wouldn't be able to pull it off as this trial and error may sometimes take years.

You can plan and quit a job you despise if you have patience and self-control.

If you feel like you're becoming less patient in recent years, you're not alone. Cultural shifts — particularly when it comes to technology — have primed us to expect immediate gratification.

When we want to read a particular book, listen to a certain song or watch a popular TV show, most of the time those things are only a few clicks away.

An evening's dinner — or a week's groceries — can appear at our door in a flash.

"So many things are available to us instantly,"

Dr. Bea says. "It's increasingly common that we get things delivered to us quickly."

And that's bad news when it comes to our ability to wait patiently.

"Our expectations go up and then our level of patience goes down," he says.

7 tips for practicing patience

So how can you strengthen your patience muscles? The first step? Let's just admit up front that it won't be much fun at first.

"If we're going to grow patience, it's going

to come from doing slightly uncomfortable things," says Dr. Bea.

Ready to work on it? Here's what he suggests if you want to become a more patient person:

Practice mindfulness. Be in the present moment, without judging. Simply sit quietly and notice your breath. Notice what distracts you from your breath, then ease yourself back into awareness of your breath.

Practice accepting your current circumstances. This may mean being stuck in traffic or stuck in a job you hate. But that doesn't mean you shouldn't try to change things if you need to. It only means accepting your experience in the moment for exactly what it is — even if it's unpleasant.

Actively build a tolerance for being a bit uncomfortable. Let other people go ahead of you in line or in traffic. Resist the urge to scratch an itch. Don't act on every impulse to check your phone.

When you're feeling rushed, consciously slow down. You don't have to feel like a hamster on a wheel all of the time. Know that you can choose slow. In our culture that prizes speed, know that there is value to be had in slow too.

Be playful. Practice acting like a kid sometimes. Sing around the house, be silly, laugh. Actively try to take yourself less seriously.

Let it feel broken. It doesn't matter whether it's a work project that's gone off the rails, a problem in your relationship or something in your home that's literally broken. Resist the urge to immediately fix everything.

Practice being a good listener. Listen carefully to what family members or other conversation partners are saying. Focus on understanding, rather than on formulating your response.

No one says increasing your patience is easy. But, with daily practice, you may find you're more calm, less frazzled and more willing to give others the benefit of the doubt — and maybe even give yourself a break once in a while, as well.

In the starting I told I will give some activities to do after each and every part to produce results.

You just DO IT, DON'T DELAY.

THERE ARE 7 PRACTICING TIPS WHICH YOU HAVE READ IN LAST 2 PAGES RIGHT! SO, DO THAT.

Practice it for next 21 days.

ALL THE BEST!

1.   HOW DO I MANAGE MY ANGER?

Why? Why? Why? Why do you get angry say the reason? Mostly teens get more anger and I don't understand why at this age schooling students get hyper tension, stress, anger, this day they are also getting heart attack in kidney and leg pain in brain.

This dialogue was used by one of my craziest friends " Krish".

I don't know what you think but one thing I will definitely say you that you are wasting your life by being Angry, you don't enjoy the current period. According to Science, your life span is going to be decrease if you be angry, sometimes it is completely fine but more that the limits will not be good to yourself. From right you start taking action on yourself. CONTOLLING YOURSELF IS TOO IMPORTANT.

Anger is a normal feeling and can be a positive emotion when it helps you work through issues or problems, whether that's at work or at home.

However, anger can become problematic if it leads to aggression, outbursts, or even physical altercations.

Anger control is important for helping you avoid saying or doing something you may regret. Before anger escalates, you can use specific strategies for controlling anger.

Here are 25 ways you can control your anger:

1. Count down

Count down (or up) to 10. If you're really mad, start at 100. In the time it takes you to count, your heart rate will slow, and your anger will likely subside.

2. Take a breather

Your breathing becomes shallower and speeds up as you grow angry. Reverse that trend (and your anger) by taking slow, deep breaths from your nose and exhaling out of your mouth for several moments.

3. Go walk around

Go for a walk, ride your bike, or hit a few golf balls. Anything that gets your limbs pumping is good for your mind and body.

4. Relax your muscles

Progressive muscle relaxation calls on you to tense and slowly relax various muscle groups in your body, one at a time. As you tense and release, take slow, deliberate breaths.

5. Repeat a mantra

Find a word or phrase that helps you calm down and refocus. Repeat that word again and again to yourself when you're upset. "Relax," "Take it easy, and "You'll be OK" are all good examples, [or] in say the dialogue of 3Idiots movie ''All Is Well''

6. Stretch

Neck rolls and shoulder rolls are good examples of nonstrenuous yoga-like movements that can help you control your body and harness your emotions. No fancy equipment required.

7. Mentally escape

Slip into a quiet room, close your eyes, and practice visualizing yourself in a relaxing scene. Focus on details in the imaginary scene: What colour is the water? How tall are the mountains? What do the chirping birds sound like? This practice can help you find calm amidst anger.

8. Play some tunes

Let music carry you away from your feelings. Put in earbuds or slip out to your car. Crank up your favourite music and hum, bop, or sashay your anger away.

9. Stop talking

When you're steamed, you may be tempted to let the angry words fly, but you're more likely to do harm than good. Pretend your lips are glued shut, just like you did as a kid. This moment without speaking will give you time to collect your thoughts.

10. Take a timeout

Give yourself a break. Sit away from others. In this quiet time, you can process events and return your emotions to neutral. You may even find this time away from others is so helpful you want to schedule it into your daily routine.

11. Take action

Harness your angry energy. Sign a petition. Write a note to an official. Do something good for someone else. Pour your energy and emotions into something that's healthy and productive.

12. Write in your journal

What you can't say, perhaps you can write. Note down what you're feeling and how you want to respond. Processing it through the written word can help you calm down and reassess the events leading up to your feelings.

13. Find the most immediate solution

You might be angry that your child has once again left their room a mess before going to visit a friend. Shut the door. You can temporarily end your anger by putting it out of your view. Look for similar resolutions in any situations.

14. Rehearse your response

Prevent an outburst by rehearsing what you're going to say or how you're going to approach the problem in the future. This rehearsal period gives you time to role-play several possible solutions, too.

15. Picture a stop sign

The universal symbol to stop can help you calm down when you're angry. It's a quick way to help you visualize the need to halt yourself, your actions, and walk away from the moment.

16. Change your routine

If your slow commute to work makes you angry before you've even had coffee, find a new route. Consider options that may take longer but leave you less upset in the end.

17. Talk to a friend

Don't stew in the events that made you angry. Help yourself process what happened by talking with a trusted, supportive friend who can possibly provide a new perspective.

18. Laugh

Nothing upends a bad mood like a good one. Diffuse your anger by looking for ways to laugh, whether that's playing with your kids, watching stand-up, or scrolling memes.

19. Practice gratitude

Take a moment to focus on what's right when everything feels wrong. Realizing how many good things you have in your life can help you neutralize anger and turn around the situation.

20. Set a timer

The first thing that comes to mind when you're angry likely isn't the thing you should say. Give yourself a set time before you respond. This time will help you be calmer and more concise.

21. Write a letter

Write a letter or email to the person that made you angry. Then, delete it. Often, expressing your emotions in some form is all you want, even if it's in something that will never be seen.

22. Imagine forgiving them

Finding the courage to forgive someone who has wronged you takes a lot of emotional skill. If you can't go that far, you can at least pretend that you're forgiving them, and you'll feel your anger slip away.

23. Practice empathy

Try to walk in the other person's shoes and see the situation from their perspective. When you tell the story or relive the events as they saw it, you may gain a new understanding and become less angry.

24. Express your anger

It's OK to say how you feel, as long as you handle it in the right way. Ask a trusted friend to help you be accountable to a calm response. Outbursts solve no problems, but mature dialogue can help reduce your stress and ease your anger. It may also prevent future problems.

25. Find a creative channel

Turn your anger into a tangible production. Consider painting, gardening, or writing poetry when you're upset. Emotions are powerful muses for creative individuals. Use yours to reduce anger.

The bottom line

Anger is a normal emotion that everyone experiences from time to time. However, if you find your anger turns to aggression or outbursts, you need to find healthy ways to deal with anger.

If these tips don't help, consider talking with your doctor. A mental health specialist or therapist can help you work through underlying factors that may contribute to anger and other emotional issues.

Anger management exercises to try

Anger outbursts can cause harm to you and the people around you.

A good way to calm anger and prevent any harm is to use anger management exercises. These techniques work by first calming you down and then helping you move forward in a positive way.

Use the following anger management exercises any time it feels your anger is overwhelming, until you feel calm:

Learn to breathe

When you're angry, you might notice your breathing gets quicker and shallower. One easy way to calm your body and reduce your anger is to slow and deepen your breathing.

Try breathing slowly into your nose and out your mouth. Breathe deeply from your belly rather than your chest. Repeat breaths as necessary.

Progressive muscle relaxation

Muscle tension is another sign of stress in the body that you may feel when you're angry.

To help calm down, you may want to try a progressive muscle relaxation technique. This involves slowly tensing and then relaxing each muscle group in the body, one at a time.

Consider starting at the top of your head and move your way to your toes, or vice versa.

Visualize yourself calm

Imagining a relaxing place may help you reduce your anger. Sit in a quiet, comfortable space from your memory and close your eyes for a few moments. Let your imagination flow.

As you think of what that relaxing place is like, think about small details. How does it smell or sound? Think about how calm and good you feel in that place.

Get moving

Besides being healthy for your bodily functions, regular exercise is very effective at reducing stress in the body and mind. Try to get some exercise every day to keep stress and anger at bay.

For a quick way to manage anger, go for a brisk walk, bike ride, run. Or do some other form of physical activity when you feel anger growing.

Recognize your triggers

Usually, people get angry about specific things over and over again. Spend some time thinking about what makes you angry. Make an effort to avoid or deal with those things, if possible.

For example, this might involve shutting the door to your child's room when they don't clean it instead of getting angry about the mess. Or it could mean using public transportation instead of driving to work if you're easily angered by traffic.

Stop and listen

When you're in an angry argument, you might find yourself jumping to conclusions and saying things that are unkind. Making an effort to stop and listen to the other person in the conversation before reacting can help your anger drop and allow you to better respond and resolve the situation.

Think carefully before replying. Tell them you need to take a step away if you feel you need to cool down before you continue the conversation.

Change your thinking

Anger can make you feel like things are worse than they really are. Reduce your anger by replacing negative thoughts with more realistic ones. You can do this by avoiding extreme words, such as "never" or "always," when you think.

Other good strategies include keeping a balanced view of the world and turning your angry demands into requests instead.

Avoid dwelling on the same things

You may rehash the same situation that made you upset over and over again, even if the problem is resolved. This is called dwelling or ruminating. Dwelling allows anger to last and could cause further arguments or other issues.

Try to move past the thing that caused your anger. Instead, try to take a look at the positive parts of the person or situation that made you upset.

Know your body

When you get angry, your body tends to get very excited. Your heart rate, blood pressure, breathing speed, and body temperature may increase. Your body also releases certain stress hormones that put your body on high alert.

Pay attention to your body when you're angry. Learn your body's anger warning signs. Next time you feel these warnings, you can step away from the situation or try a relaxation technique.

The bottom line

Anger is a common and useful emotion everyone experiences. It's also possible for anger to become overwhelming and cause problems sometimes.

Anger management exercises are useful tools that can help identify and manage anger in a productive way. Getting expert help is a good way to address anger that's interfering with your quality of life.

1.3. HOW CAN I BE MORE SELF-AWARE?

[from this page the font size will be changing to little bigger for better experience.]

Self-awareness is being intensely aware of why you do things in the first place.

The more awareness you have of the 'why', the more you will know what works for you and what doesn't.

Most of my life decisions in life were not made because of my confidence in the decision.

They were made because of my awareness of my situation.

I didn't know whether those decisions were right or wrong.

However, not making those decisions despite being aware of all other options was certainly the wrong decision.

Decisions are not for decoding destinations. Decisions are far deciphering the path you want to demonstrate next.

If everyone did it, it wouldn't need to be said.

Not everyone exercises. Thus, it needs to be said more often.

Not everyone spends time with their team. Thus, the best leaders say it more often.

Not everyone spends time journaling. Thus, the wisest minds help us to get into the habit.

Everyone watches TV, it needn't to be said. Everyone needs pizza it needn't to be said. Everyone has a smartphone it needn't to be said, Possess one.

The things that are the most important and the least practised, are the things that are said. **Doing the things that are the most important are the things that make you important.**

Fear has led to more procrastination than laziness ever will.

You don't procrastinate because you are lazy. You procrastinate because you are scared.

What if I fail?

What if I succeed?

What if my life is sorted after this?

What if I have to face rejection?

You aren't lazy. You simply aren't ready to meet yourself on the other side.

Because you won't have those reasons then, living a fearless life isn't what you are used to.

Unless you know why you do something in the first place, you won't be able to change it.

Think about failures.

Everyone in the world fails.

But not everyone succeeds.

Why is it then that we call failures stepping stones to success?

Because the one who succeed eventually after failing reflected on their failures.

Instead of quickly moving on, they asked themselves multiple questions:

- What I thought was true but now I know is not?
- What I thought was false, but now I know he is not?
- What is this trying to teach me?
- What will I change from tomorrow, basis the responses arrow?

But you still wonder how this works?

It works because reflection makes us pause. But we all hate to reflect, to pause.

We are scared of what we might discover when we sit to reflect.

This is true for life.

Whenever you feel stuck, feel helpless, feel directionless, sit with yourself.

Meditate on what you need to do in life in order to move ahead.

You **will** find an answer.

The answer will not be the one you like, but it will certainly be the one you need.

Like how you like the pizza and burger and other fast foods but you don't like the green leafy vegetables and healthy foods, **same in that way this happens.**

Hey most of the people get comfortable avoiding rather than being aware. Is that the right way to put it?

Yes. It's the sad truth.

The answer will require effort.

It will require commitment.

It will also require you to shift your way of living and behaviour.

That is why it is going to be uncomfortable.

But is that the only way to become self-aware?

What do you think?

There are lot of people who reach out to me saying,

'I am confused. what should I do'

The last thing a good person does is serve answers on a platter.

I ask them, 'what's stopping you from doing what you know you should do?'

Now the question comes:

If everyone knows what they should do, why don't they do it?

Fear. Fear. Fear.

- Fear of failure.
- Fear of rejection.
- Fear of success.
- Fear of the unknown.
- Fear of being compared to others.
- Fear of reprimand.

That fear stops them from asking themselves: What is really stopping me from facing that fear?

The moment they ask themselves this question they take the first steps towards awareness.

Then it becomes a journey.

Just like the journey of fitness.

You have to undertake it daily to call yourself fit.

It is a journey, not a destination.

No one ever say 'I am fit'; they can only claim 'I remain fit'.

The day you end the journey, you eventually stop being fit.

So, many people are caught in a rut, and still complain about their life not changing. How is it possible that they know **how to get out and yet they continue to live in the rut?**

Here is the shocking truth.

The rut is their comfort.

Because it allows them to complaint.

It allows them to believe everything is someone else's fault.

It allows them to believe that the world owes them something.

The ones not in a relationship thinks those who are in relationships oh them something. The ones working in a company taking the company owes them something.

Their belief system is driven by the fact that has someone else behave the right way or had something else worked out for them, there world would have been a better one.

How does one even realise this and become self-aware?

When someone is ready to take the **journey** of self-awareness, they **will recognise** the need for it.

It will emerge by itself you cannot push someone to be **self-aware.**

Hey I think this journey of self-awareness is best undertaken as early as possible. Overtime it will become a habit and next thing you - **know facing the truth is the default mode for you.**

1.4. HOW CAN I LIVE BY MYSELF?

To live by yourself is both magical yet miserable, don't you think? Magical because you experience freedom from the first time.

Miserable because sometimes you end up misusing that freedom or mismanaging it. I wonder if there is a middle way.

When you start living by yourself you experience 3 aspects of your life – money, health end relationships.

Let's start with money.

When you were at your home, you never thought about something as fundamental as which toothpaste to use, what utensils/ appliances to have, what to cook, how the house get cleaned everyday – all of it happened without you being given aware of anything. But when you move out of your home for school or college, you will have no choice but to make all these decisions from day one.

You don't even know where to start. That's why this book is named <u>Do it Don't Delay</u>.

By creating a budget.

A budget for your money – base it on what you need to do, what you want to do and what you have to do.

What you need to do are your needs. Your essentials.

This includes your food, your bills, your help, your rent.

Everything that you need to spend to just survive.

What you want to do are your desires.

This includes, your parties, your vacations, your phones.

Everything that you wish to spend on to enjoy your life.

What you have to do are your investments.

Investments such like to create content on Instagram, YouTube, and other social media handles.

Investing yourself by taking some courses which will develop your skill set.

These investments will be slightly high cost. But later on, you may get better results and earn for your surviving and for your desires.

Planning is easy

Execution requires discipline.

The biggest thing that goes for a toss when we live by ourselves is health.

When we are at home, we used to think that are parents are restrictive and acting miserly by not allowing us to order food.

All we had everyday were boring homemade meals.

But they were simple making sure that you ate healthy while not spending unnecessarily.

You do order food day couple of times a week since I live away from my parents.

Hey the things that you say about becoming unhealthy – I don't see.

I still look the same as I used to.

The truth about bad health habit sees that you do not see any effect of the abuse in your age.

It is when you enter your 20s that you start to experience the consequences of your decisions. Some of those consequences may set you back by decades.

So, do you mean that you should not enjoy your food?

must You absolutely.

But if you are eating only for enjoyment, then its anything but enjoyment. You need to reflect upon this further.

While you do, let me move on to the 3rd aspect that becomes our responsibility when we start living by ourselves – **relationships.**

Most of your relationships while staying with parents were relationships by birth {your relatives} or those that were supervised by your parents {your friends}. You never truly experience independence in your relationships.

But now you will.

Hey this independence can get to our head.

we may tend to get into relationships that harm us.

How do you know that?

You will start spending time with people because of how they make you look in front of others instead of who they truly are.

You begin to talk about people and not ideas.

How do you avoid these relationship mistakes?

You start with not rebounding immediately after a relationship failure.

Rather, you stop, pause, and reflect upon why you got into that relationship in the first place.

What unfulfilled need of yours did that relationship fulfil?

The level of awareness comes only when you spend time with yourself, which will eventually make you better at making choices in relationships.

People aren't 'good' or 'bad' per se; someone who is an Angel to one may be a nightmare to another.

Our temperament defines how our relationships makes us feel.

All of these seem so overwhelming. Why is it so important to take care of yourself so much when you live by yourself?

Because you will be by yourself now for the rest of your life. Even when you form other relationships, you will only truly have yourself to call upon. Everyone else is merely an observer. But they can never know what you are going through.

Until you do not learn how to live by, with yourself, you will continue to look for others in your life to complete your life.

I am the only one for myself and you too.

I find that living by yourself bring with it a lot of FOMO.

You may have some questions regarding this topic like:

What if I do not go out and post that food picture on my Instagram?

I do not have the money to go on a trip with my friends but what do I tell them?

Will I be the party spoiler if I choose to take care of my health and not it what we order at the restaurant?

Will it affect my relationships as well?

These questions keep bothering you.

Living by yourself will eventually teach you how to deal with these questions.

Let's say your friends want you to eat out. You eat something before you go and that fills you up. So, when you get to the restaurant, you eat in a limited manner.

Surprise, surprise: overtime, everyone will come to accept that you eat only this much.

If you are invited for a vacation, you want to go but also you want to take care of your monthly budget; you go for 2-3 days instead of the entire vacation.

Go to the end so that no one can force you to stay longer.

There are no straight forward answers. We all make them up along the way as you will too.

Becoming like this is little weird but I know that you will enjoy the process.

You tag me on Instagram if you enjoy the book at present.

But I know it before, you enjoy this book, **definitely we will enjoy it's my guarantee.**